Contents

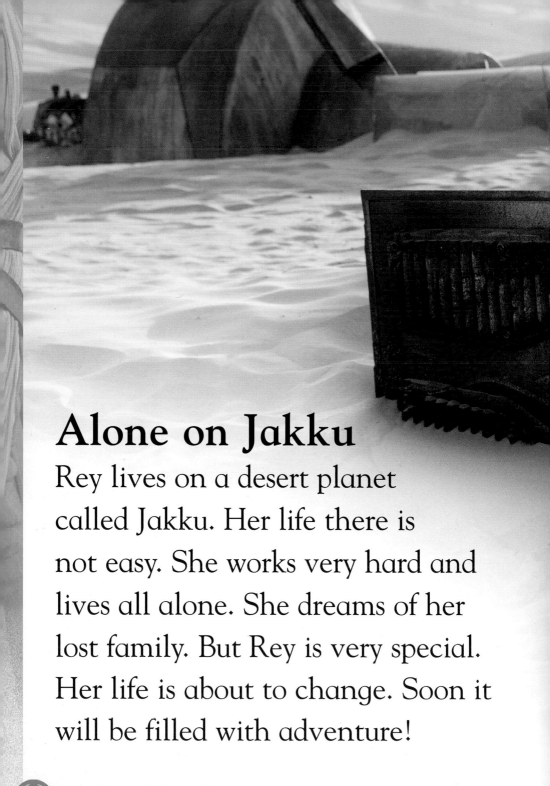

Alone on Jakku

Rey lives on a desert planet
called Jakku. Her life there is
not easy. She works very hard and
lives all alone. She dreams of her
lost family. But Rey is very special.
Her life is about to change. Soon it
will be filled with adventure!

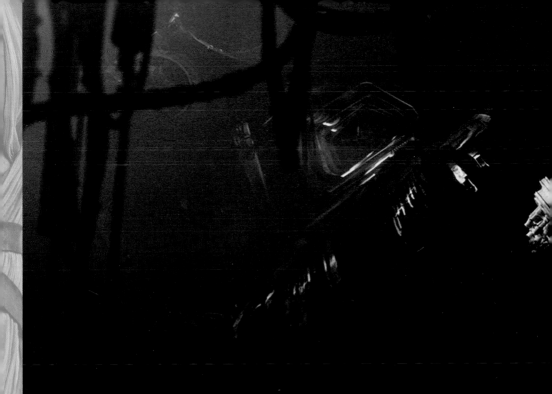

Scavenging

Rey works as a scavenger. Every day
she treks into junkfields. She looks
for parts from old ships that can still
be used. Rey can trade these parts
for food. Her job is dangerous, but
she is tough and brave.

Rey puts the old parts in a net on her speeder.

READY FOR ACTION!

Every day on Jakku is a fight for survival. Rey is always prepared to face the hot desert sun and any sly scavengers!

Dark goggles

Sack holds tools

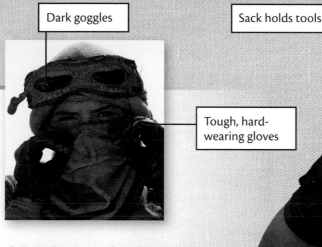

Tough, hard-wearing gloves

SPECIAL CLOTHING

Rey wears special clothing to protect herself when she is in the open desert.

DATA FILE

Age: 19

Species: Human

Height: 1.7 m (5 ft 7 in)

Location: Jakku

Job: Scavenger

Weapon: Quarterstaff

Quarterstaff for self-defense

Tough traveler's boots

9

Niima Outpost

The largest town on Jakku is Niima Outpost. This is where Rey brings her junk to be sold. Niima Outpost is very hot and dusty.

There are lots of mean and smelly creatures around. One of the meanest creatures is Unkar Plutt. He trades junk for food.

Unkar Plutt

Home

Rey's home is a broken, old vehicle called an AT-AT. It lies on its side in the sand. Inside, Rey spends her time fixing junk. There is a hammock for her to sleep on when she is tired from her work.

Rey makes sure that her home is protected even while she sleeps. She has set clever traps to keep other scavengers out.

REY'S SPEEDER

Rey is very good at fixing and building machines. She built her speeder out of old parts. It is her pride and joy!

Fuel tank

Rear balance panel

Footrest

Start-up motor

Wires taken from
X-wing starship

Safety grille

Exhaust vent

Little friend

Rey does not have many friends, but she is kind. When she first sees the droid BB-8 she knows she needs to help him. A Teedo scavenger is trying to capture him. Rey saves BB-8 and fixes his broken antenna. Meeting BB-8 changes Rey's life forever.

The Teedo scavenger rides a creature called a luggabeast.

Self-defense

Jakku is a very dangerous place.
Rey has no one there to protect her
against thugs and thieves. She has
learned how to defend herself.

Rey is a skilled fighter. She uses a
weapon called a quarterstaff, which
she carries on her back. Rey does
not realize that her quick reactions
come from the Force.

SURVIVAL GUIDE

Rey does not know how she came to live on Jakku. All she knows is that she needs to survive. Here are her tips for staying alive.

Survival tip ①

Protect your body! Shield yourself from the heat and sand, and drink lots of water.

Survival tip 2

Do your homework!
Learn which ship parts
are the most valuable
for scavenging.

Survival tip 3

**Don't trust
anyone!** There is
no time for
friends on Jakku.

Wall markings
Every night Rey makes
a scratch on her wall. It
marks another day that she
has survived on Jakku.

Finn

When Rey meets Finn she thinks he is part of the Resistance. He does not tell her the truth. Finn used to be a stormtrooper for the First Order!

He ran away because the First Order was evil. Now the First Order is chasing him. Finn lies to Rey because he wants her to like him. Rey helps him escape from Jakku.

Piloting skills

Rey has always liked exploring old starships. She has found out how they work. She even knows how to fly them! When Rey and Finn have to leave Jakku, she finds a starship called the *Millennium Falcon* to fly away in. They escape thanks to Rey's amazing piloting skills.

Quick thinking

Rathtars are big, slimy beasts. It is
not easy to outsmart one. When
Finn is grabbed by a rathtar, Rey has
to think fast. The rathtar is too big
for her to fight. She must find
another way to save her friend.

Rey finds the ship's control
panel. She presses a button
    that shuts a door on the
        rathtar. Its tentacles
            are sliced off, and
            Finn is saved!

Famous ship

The *Millennium Falcon* is a famous starship. It used to belong to a smuggler named Han Solo and his Wookiee friend, Chewbacca. They flew it in many space battles before Rey was even born. Now it is very old and can sometimes break down. Han is amazed that Rey knows just how to fix it!

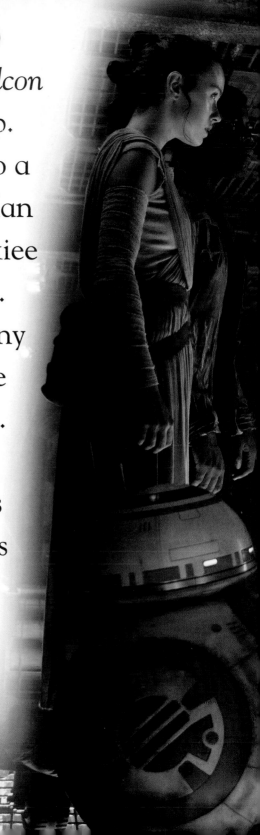

THE FORCE

An invisible energy called the Force flows through all living things. Rey can feel the Force. She must learn to control its power and keep to the right side!

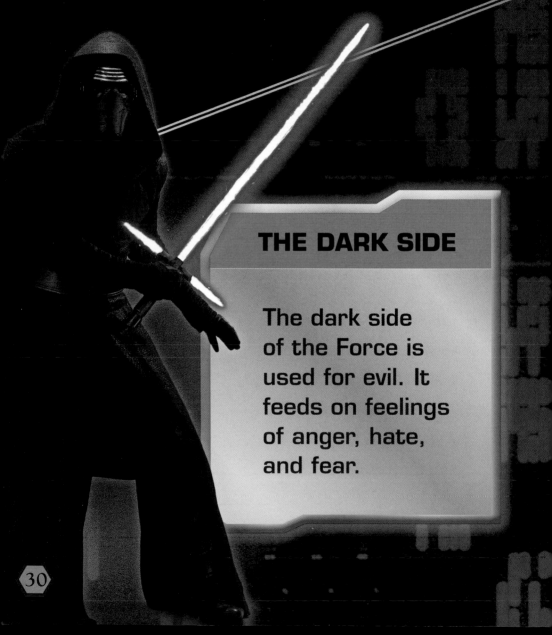

THE DARK SIDE

The dark side of the Force is used for evil. It feeds on feelings of anger, hate, and fear.

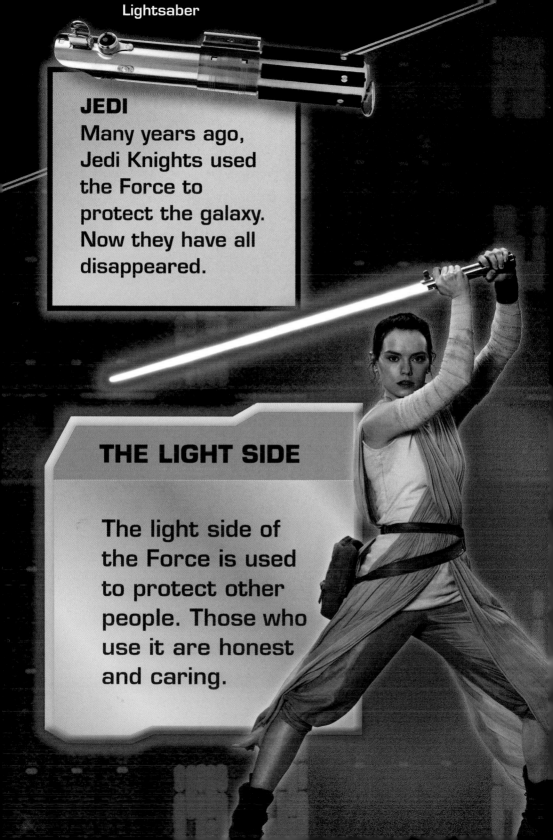

JEDI

Many years ago, Jedi Knights used the Force to protect the galaxy. Now they have all disappeared.

THE LIGHT SIDE

The light side of the Force is used to protect other people. Those who use it are honest and caring.

Evil enemy

Kylo Ren is a terrifying
warrior of the First Order.
He wears a dark cape
and scary mask to hide
who he really is. His
Force powers are very
strong. He can destroy
anyone who gets in his
way. Kylo Ren wants to
take over the galaxy.
Can Rey and her
friends stop him?

Lightsaber vision

Rey finds a lightsaber hidden in a box on the planet Takodana. When she touches it, she has a shocking vision! She sees images from the past. She also sees things that will happen in the future!

Maz Kanata explains to Rey what
her vision means. Rey can feel the
Force! She must
help save
the galaxy.

THE RESISTANCE

The Resistance is a group that protects the galaxy from the First Order. It may not have many ships or weapons, but it has plenty of brave members. General Leia is eager to have Rey's help.

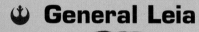 **General Leia**

- Brave and wise Resistance leader
- Plans all Resistance operations

Han Solo

- Helps whenever the Resistance needs him
- Not afraid to face great danger

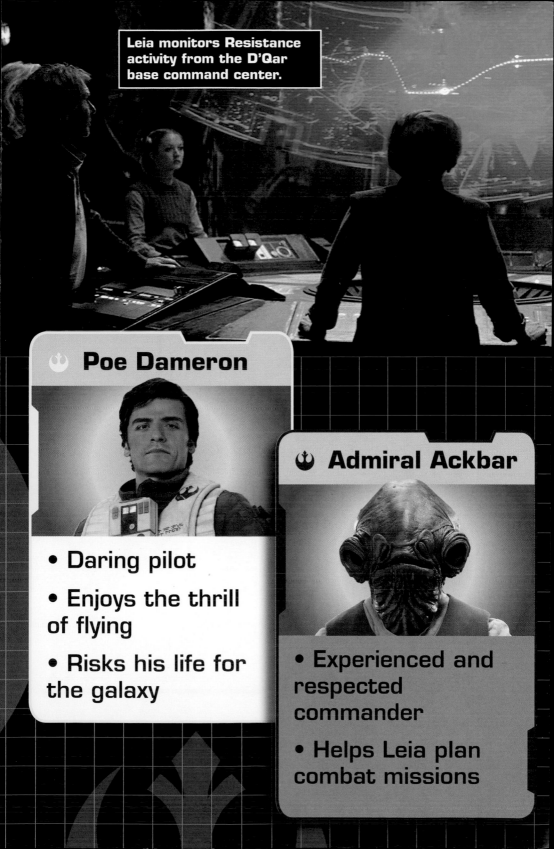

Leia monitors Resistance activity from the D'Qar base command center.

Poe Dameron

- Daring pilot
- Enjoys the thrill of flying
- Risks his life for the galaxy

Admiral Ackbar

- Experienced and respected commander
- Helps Leia plan combat missions

Force powers

Rey's Force powers are tested for
the first time on Starkiller Base.
Rey has been captured by Kylo Ren.
He wants to read Rey's mind.

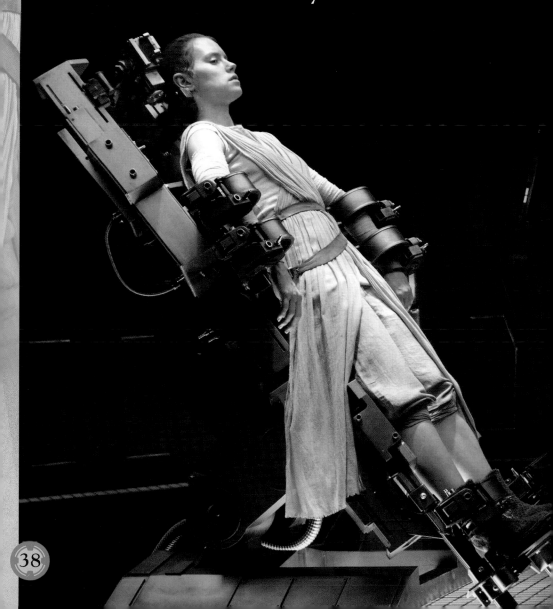

Rey uses the Force to stop Kylo Ren
from seeing all of her thoughts.
She is able to read his mind instead!
Rey is starting to realize how
strong her Force powers really are.

Lightsaber duel

Kylo Ren is not finished
with Rey. He wants to
destroy her! Rey fights
Kylo Ren in a fierce
lightsaber duel. She has
grown very strong with
the Force. She almost
defeats her powerful
enemy! Kylo Ren is
able to escape this time.
But next time they meet,
Rey's Force powers will
be even stronger!

Quiz

1. What planet does Rey live on?

2. Where does Rey bring her junk to be sold?

3. What old vehicle does Rey use as her home?

4. Who does Rey save from a Teedo scavenger?

5. Why did Finn leave the First Order?

6. What is the name of the starship that Rey flies off Jakku?

7. Which side of the Force feeds on anger, hate, and fear?

8. What does Rey find hidden on Takodana?

9. Who is the leader of the Resistance?

Answers on page 48

Glossary

Droid
A kind of robot

Duel
A battle fought between
two people

Experienced
Having gained a lot
of knowledge over
a long time

The First Order
A powerful evil army

The Force
A mysterious energy
that flows through
the galaxy

Galaxy
A group of millions of
stars and planets

General
Someone who leads
soldiers in battle

Jedi
A warrior who uses the
light side of the Force
to do good

Junkfields
A place where there
is a lot of junk to
search through

Lightsaber
A sword that has a
glowing laser blade

Outsmart
To defeat someone
or something by
being clever

The Resistance
A group that defends
the galaxy from the
First Order

Scavenger
Someone who searches
through worthless junk
to find useful things

Smuggler
Someone who transports things secretly to make money from selling them

Starkiller Base
The First Order's headquarters

Starship
A vehicle used in space

Stormtrooper
A soldier of the First Order

Survival
Staying alive in a difficult situation

Terrifying
Very scary and frightening

Valuable
Worth a lot of money

Vision
A dreamlike picture seen in the mind

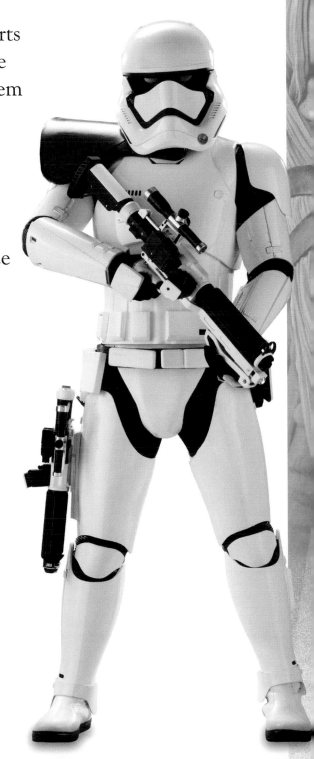

Guide for Parents

This book is part of an exciting four-level reading series for children, developing the habit of reading widely for both pleasure and information. These chapter books have a compelling main narrative to suit your child's reading ability. Each book is designed to develop your child's reading skills, fluency, grammar awareness, and comprehension in order to build confidence and engagement when reading.

Ready for a *Level 2* book

YOUR CHILD SHOULD

- be familiar with using beginning letter sounds and context clues to figure out unfamiliar words.
- be aware of the need for a slight pause at commas and a longer one at periods.
- alter his/her expression for questions and exclamations.

A VALUABLE AND SHARED READING EXPERIENCE

For many children, reading requires much effort, but adult participation can make this both fun and easier. So here are a few tips on how to use this book with your child.

TIP 1 Check out the contents together before your child begins:

- read the text about the book on the back cover.
- flip through the book and stop to chat about the contents page together to heighten your child's interest and expectation.
- make use of unfamiliar or difficult words on the page in a brief discussion.
- chat about the nonfiction reading features used in the book, such as headings, captions, lists, or charts.

TIP 2 Support your child as he/she reads the story pages:

- give the book to your child to read and turn the pages.
- where necessary, encourage your child to break a word into syllables, sound out each one, and then flow the syllables together. Ask him/her to reread the sentence to check the meaning.
- when there's a question mark or an exclamation mark, encourage your child to vary his/her voice as he/she reads the sentence. Demonstrate how to do this if it is helpful.

TIP 3 Chat at the end of each page:

- ask questions about the text and the meaning of the words used. These help to develop comprehension skills and awareness of the language used.

A FEW ADDITIONAL TIPS

- Always encourage your child to try reading difficult words by themselves. Praise any self-corrections, for example, "I like the way you sounded out that word and then changed the way you said it, to make sense."
- Try to read together everyday. Reading little and often is best. These books are divided into manageable chapters for one reading session. However, after 10 minutes, only keep going if your child wants to read on.
- Read other books of different types to your child just for enjoyment and information.

Series consultant, **Dr. Linda Gambrell**, Distinguished Professor of Education at Clemson University, has served as President of the National Reading Conference, the College Reading Association, and the International Reading Association.

Index

Answers to the quiz on pages 42 and 43:
1. Jakku 2. Niima Outpost 3. An AT-AT 4. BB-8
5. He realized it was evil 6. *The Millennium Falcon*
7. The dark side 8. A lightsaber 9. General Leia